I WANT TO BE BILINGUAL!

Written by Adam Beck

Illustrated by Pavel Goldaev

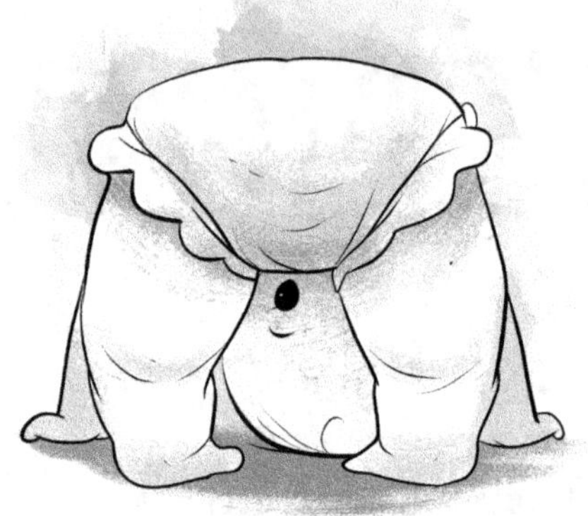

I WANT TO BE BILINGUAL!
Copyright © 2019 by Adam Beck

Published by Bilingual Adventures
For inquiries, contact Adam Beck: adam@bilingualmonkeys.com

Website: http://bilingualmonkeys.com
Forum: http://bilingualzoo.com
Facebook: https://www.facebook.com/bilingualmonkeys

First Edition, 2019

ISBN 978-4-908629-04-4

Hello! Nice to meet you! I'm your new baby!

Thanks for inviting me to join your family! You guys seem really friendly and I'm looking forward to a fun childhood with lots of toys! Hurray!

Before we get started, though, there's something important I want to talk to you about. Seriously, this is something that might even be more important than toys. I know we just met and everything, but I want to ask you guys a big favor...

I WANT
TO BE
BILINGUAL!

And I want a pony, too,
but let's talk about that later.

You see, being bilingual would be good for me, I think. I hear it's good for the brain—it makes the brain stronger, from childhood to old age. Who doesn't want a good, strong brain that lasts a whole lifetime, right?

Being bilingual could be good for my future, too. I'll have the chance to make more friends and maybe even get a good job. After you've spent all your money on me, I can help you when you're old and poor.

Plus, I'm not sure yet if you guys each speak a different language or what, but if you do, I want to learn them both. I mean, unless I can speak the languages that are a part of you, I don't think I can really know you as well as I'd like.

And if I can't speak those languages, it'll be a lot harder for me to communicate with my own grandparents and get them to buy me stuff when we go shopping.

The thing is, guys, I'm still in diapers, you know.

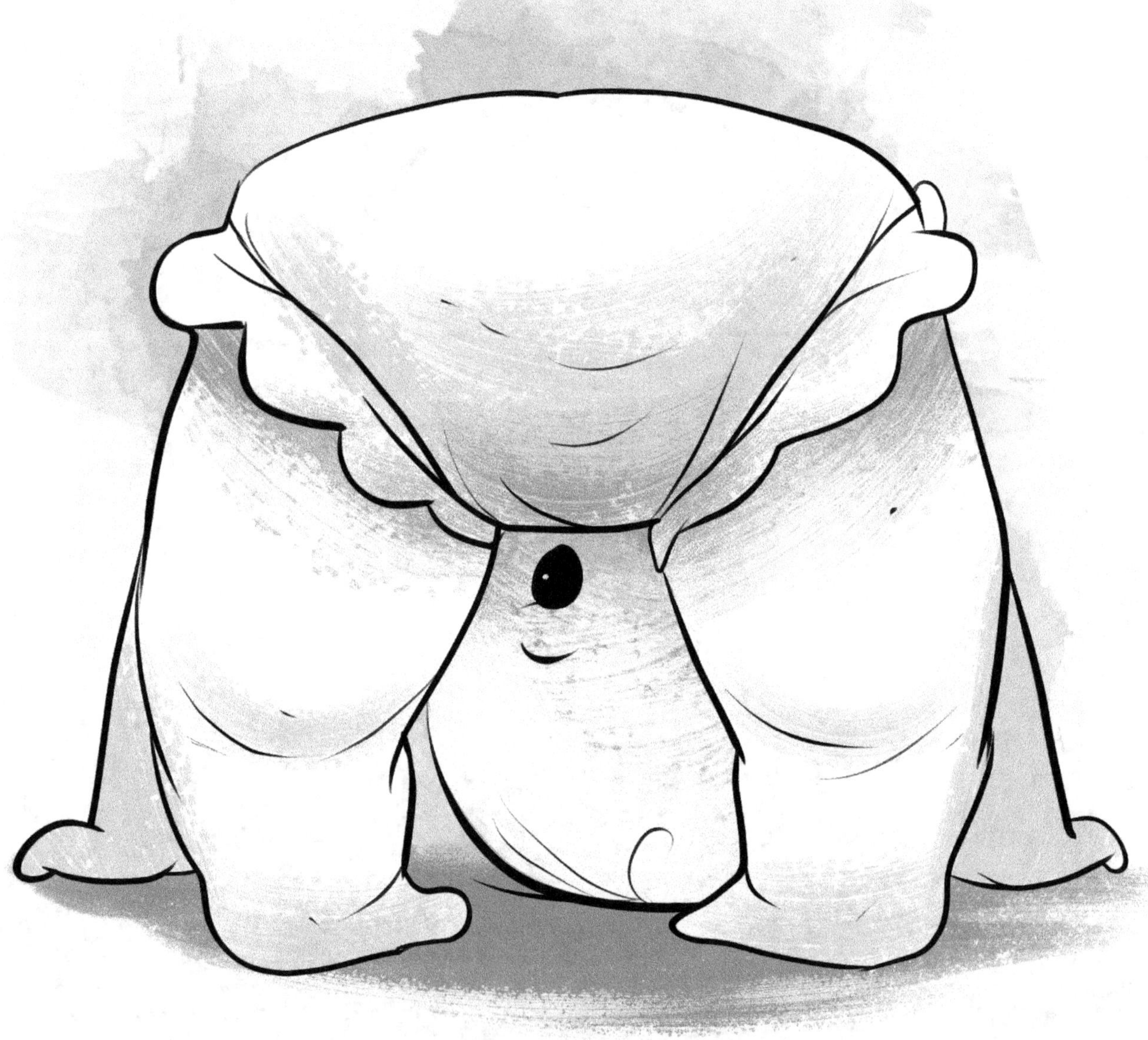

You can't expect me to become bilingual all by myself.

The key question is...

What can you do to help me be bilingual?

Well, the most important thing, really, is to make sure I hear both languages a lot, especially the one that isn't the main language where we live. And don't just plop me in front of a TV—that won't work. This input stuff has to come mostly from real-live people.

So talk to me a lot, even though I can't really reply yet. And find other real-live people who can talk to me, too. The more you guys talk to me, the more I'll be able to talk to you, when I'm ready.

And by the way, I'm sorry about all those temper tantrums I'll throw when I'm older. Don't take it personally when I scream at you or even bite you.

Little kids are like that.

Please read to me every day, too. Year after year. If you read to me in both languages—again, especially in the language we don't hear as much outside the house— that will really help. I'll learn the languages better, and I'll learn to read on my own more easily, too.

And when we snuggle up together to read, this will make
us feel closer and books will become special things to me.

Just be careful with those chunky board books.
I don't think I'd like one of those dropped on my head.

This means you'll have to get into the habit of looking for books and other stuff, like music and games, to help me become bilingual. The more books and things we have in the house, the more fun we can have together and the more progress I'll make.

So lots of input like this—talking to me, reading to me, playing with me—is the main thing. And if there's not enough of it in one of our languages, it will probably be harder for me to speak that language when I start talking back to you.

But it's not just input. I need a lot of that, day after day, but I also need...well, I need a real *need* to use both languages. If it seems I can communicate with you guys well enough in just one language, I might not feel much need to speak the other one. So make sure I feel a strong need to use both languages, okay?

Those are the most important things. Lots of playful input in both languages, and especially in the language that isn't used so much around here. Plus, a real need to use that language so I don't just rely on the other one to communicate.

It sounds pretty simple, I guess. But actually, it might be hard for you to stay active each day to support my second language, the one I won't have the chance to use as often. You'll probably get tired sometimes—grown-ups are like that. But guys, please keep doing your best.

I should warn you, I'll probably get tired of this sometimes, too. But even when I moan about it, like complaining when I have to do homework in two languages and my friends only have to do homework in one, just keep going, just keep trying.

Because the truth is, I really *do* want to be bilingual. Even when I forget this, and I start moaning and complaining, it's still true. Deep down, it will always be true.

And when I'm grown up, and I'm bilingual, I'll be really glad you never gave up on this goal. If you give up, I think we'll both regret it.

Thanks a lot, guys. I'm happy we're finally together.
I know everything won't always be as much fun as
sucking my thumb, but I'm excited about the future.
I'm excited about being bilingual.

And no matter what, let's love each other,
day and night, like there's no tomorrow.

Now can we talk about toys? And that pony?

Author's note

As the baby was just stressing, the two most important factors in raising a bilingual (or multilingual) child are these:

1. Exposure

2. Need

The two "core conditions" of exposure and need—ample exposure to the minority language* and a genuine need to actively use this language for communication—are at the very heart of success and should be kept firmly in mind throughout the bilingual journey.

Though both conditions are important, language exposure—as much and as interactive as possible—is particularly important and the top priority. As a general rule, the more input that your child receives in the minority language, both from you and from other sources of exposure, the more progress he or she will make over the years of childhood. Fundamentally, language exposure is the one absolute requirement for every family with a bilingual dream.

While ample language exposure is the first, all-important condition, a genuine need for the minority language is often also required in order for the child to actively use this language. In some cases, such as when the child is "conditioned," from an early age, to communicate in the minority language with a parent who is also proficient in the majority language, this conditioning can make up for the lack of real need. But broadly speaking, if the child doesn't feel a strong need to speak the minority language, he or she will more likely rely on the majority language to communicate.

*The minority language is the language that is not the main language of the community; that main language is termed the majority language. The minority language generally requires considerably more effort to cultivate than the majority language, which is fostered—even without much exposure at home—through the immersion of school and society.

When these two factors—exposure and need—are in sufficient supply, steady and satisfying progress will unfold in the child's language development.

However, when there are shortcomings in one or both of these areas, the child may not yet have gained adequate ability, or feel enough need, to make use of the minority language as actively as the parents hope. In other words, the child's ability in the second language is still more passive: he or she might comprehend the language reasonably well, but is not yet able, or willing, to use it actively.

A situation of passive ability can be discouraging, but it's important to recognize that this ability is also a significant achievement and can still be "activated" by strengthening the two "core conditions" of exposure and need. Whether at the beginning of your bilingual journey, or at any point along the long road of language acquisition, exposure and need will always be the main factors for fostering success.

As you embark on your bilingual adventure, I encourage you to stay as mindful and proactive as you realistically can, right from the start and straight through the childhood years, when it comes to providing your child with language exposure and nurturing the need for its use. Your patient and persistent efforts, pursued day by day with a playful and persevering spirit, will surely result in the joyful success that you seek.

Adam Beck
Author of *Maximize Your Child's Bilingual Ability: Ideas and inspiration for even greater success and joy raising bilingual kids*

About the author

Adam Beck is the founder of the popular blog Bilingual Monkeys and the lively forum The Bilingual Zoo. His book *Maximize Your Child's Bilingual Ability* is a uniquely empowering guide to the bilingual journey that has been praised worldwide by leaders in the field of child bilingualism and parents raising bilingual and multilingual children.

He is also the author of *How I Lost My Ear,* an epic, laugh-out-loud novel for both children and adults, to read alone or read aloud. Critics have called Adam Beck "a master storyteller" and the book "an extraordinary imaginative achievement."

He has lived in Hiroshima, Japan since 1996 and has two children who are bilingual in Japanese and English.

Bilingual Monkeys: http://bilingualmonkeys.com

The Bilingual Zoo: http://bilingualzoo.com

Email: adam@bilingualmonkeys.com

www.ingramcontent.com/pod-product-compliance
Lightning Source LLC
LaVergne TN
LVHW080613200726
843509LV00007B/299